Who are these broads?

MARYJANE FAHEY

Maryjane Fahey is a writer, designer, and former serial monogamist living in NYC. Her specialty has been journalism and editorial design, including the redesign of *BusinessWeek* and the *Boston Globe*, and the launch of *Women's Health*. MJ is **MJ** a graduate of the School of Visual Arts and Newark School of Fine Arts. Newark has an art school, that's right — it's not just where the airport is. She has every intention of continuing her new career as a writer and absolutely no intention of being dumped again.

CARYN BETH ROSENTHAL

Caryn Beth Rosenthal, a former Benny Hill Babe, is an actress/writer who hails from Jacksonville, Florida. Her credits include animation, sketch, soaps, and regional and Off-Broadway theater, including a solo show she wrote and **CB** performs in called *Getting Over Mark*, as well as numerous voice-overs and commercials. CB lives in NYC with her loyal mutt, Jax, an 8-pounder on wheels who thinks he's a 200-pound four-legged rottweiler. His credits are too numerous to mention.

WWW.DUMPED411.COM

We just **LOVE** these people for lovin' us!

"A kick-ass book about picking your ass up when you're down . . . These gals are the best coaches – and best friends – that you need."

— **Jill Conner Browne, author**
Sweet Potato Queens' Book of Love
#1 *New York Times* Best Seller

"DUMPED is a hilarious, irreverent, and empowering (but not in a gross way) guide to getting over the guy and getting a life. You will laugh, nod, and finally delete that jerk from your contacts."

— **Amy Sohn, columnist/author**
***New York Magazine, New York Post* &**
Sex and the City: Kiss and Tell
New York Times Best Seller

". . . After reading DUMPED, you'll wish you were dumped yourself just so you can join their gang of self-empowered babes."

— **Lewis Schiff, coauthor**
The Middle-Class Millionaire

". . . Read Maryjane Fahey & Caryn Beth Rosenthal's funny, yet spot-on practical guide to getting over the jerk."

— **Tracey Jackson, author/screenwrit**
***Between a Rock and a Hot Place* &**
Confessions of a Shopaholic

Contents

Chapter 1 HOW DUMPED CAME ABOUT 9

Chapter 2 OUR STORIES 13

Chapter 3 TAKE CARE OF YOURSELF 19

Chapter 4 CLOSURE — HUH? 33

Chapter 5 RED FLAGS 45

Chapter 6 LET IT GO 61

Chapter 7 BE OPEN 71

Chapter 8 YOU DESERVE A SEX LIFE 83

Chapter 9 TURNING POINTS 91

Chapter 10 HELLO, GORGEOUS 97

Chapter 11 NOW GET YOUR ASS OUT!! 113

Chapter 12 RELAPSES 127

Chapter 13 THAT JOY THANG 139

NEVER THOUGHT YOU'D BE THERE, HUH? You're suddenly alone because of a breakup, divorce, dumping, you dumping — whatever, we really don't care. The point is that now you are at a… crossroads. Congratulations!!! You are now the proud owner of a brand-spankin'-new lease on life! This is that incredible opportunity you've been waiting for! Guess what?! You no longer have to put up with his shit anymore! Way to go! You can actually do this thing called… raise your standards! *And* it won't cost you a dime! Wooohooo!

Listen, we don't all get paid to take off for a year and head for Italy, India, or Indonesia to "find ourselves" as precious Liz did in *Eat Pray Love.* Some of us actually have to work because we have kids, rents, mortgages, taxes, waxings, happy hours... Kind of tough to do all that *and* get over an ex.

So, here's our cheap, easy, and quick way to recover — because we know you don't have the time, money, or energy to waste on that ex.

CHAPTER 1

HOW DUMPED CAME ABOUT

ONE FOURTH OF JULY WEEKEND I was alone at my sister's romantic country house.
My partner opted to visit his 80-year-old mommy following a monthlong business trip to Europe. Caryn was spending that same July 4th weekend solo as well because her boyfriend was visiting *his* 90-year-old mommy. FYI: Don't just walk — *run* from the mommy bullshit.

I HAD MY FAVORITE RED, white, and blue party dress on and the asshole ditched me. So typical. When he returned on July 5th, I finally dumped his ass. It was the last straw. Most liberating July 4th weekend I've ever had. Talk about your fireworks.

SIX DAYS AFTER THAT, I got the unexpected dump from my partner of seven years.

Our universes collided and we joined forces in recovery.

TOOK US A FRICKIN' YEAR, which is nuts. We did everything we could possibly do to get over our exes, and it was a bitch of a year. We read, Netflixed®, taped all the "experts." Saw shrinks, life coaches, trainers, Oprah, astrologists, gurus . . . You name it, we did it, and it *still* took us forever to get on with our lives.

So folks, we did the grunt work and got it down so you can do it in half that time. We are your two wise girlfriends in one little book ready to help you get your head outta your ass — and we ain't takin' no for an answer.

Life is not a dress rehearsal! Whatcha waitin' for, ladies??

LET'S
PARTY!

CHAPTER 2

OUR STORIES

MY EX WAS 15 YEARS YOUNGER, but since he acted like an old coot 25 years older, the math worked. The first few years were pretty damn great. Aren't they always? I loved his combination of girly ways and sensitive art banter. I tried to ignore his penchant for three bottles of wine a night, the mommy addiction, and a rapidly expanding midsection. Ironically, I thought his love affair with his mother guaranteed me a safe voyage into old age . . . That seems hilarious to me now.

Seven years into it, I had a meltdown during the financial crisis. I got needy and scared as I watched my business crash and my savings dissipate. I assumed we were life partners and that I could lean on him emotionally. Instead, he ate, drank, and traveled — basically, anything to avoid *SEX.* I got dumped in a phone call.

I realized after the breakup that I was consumed with giving him all the advice I needed to give myself. My fears about money got in the way of believing in myself and pursuing my own dreams. Now, I heed my own advice and live a life that is calmer, fuller, and less frantic. It's the life I've wanted for years.

The first step to my recovery: keeping a journal! Write down what you're going through. It's cathartic and revealing.

CB **A JOURNAL WORKED FOR MJ** — but that's not my style. If I were to write down all that crap, I'd immediately crumple it into a ball and chuck it.

My guy was 20 years older and separated. We had a great time. Lots of fun. Never wanted to marry him or have his kids or even live with him. Basically, I'm what you'd call an old man's wet dream. It was the "perfect" relationship for both of us. After five years he finally got a divorce and dumped me for the first time. There were several more dumps. I lost count. He'd want me back after a few weeks and I'd go. Five years later, on that symbolic July 4th weekend, I left *HIM*. He didn't try to stop me. It was over. I felt such relief the first month. Like I was shot out of a cannon or dropped out of a plane without a parachute — and I hate to fly. It felt exhilarating. One month later, as I was walking on Houston Street with my friend Dana, I had a breakdown and realized I was not okay after all. Started therapy once a month (think of it as having a massage) and started saying "yes" to everything. I began to dig deeper as to what a woman is supposed to do when the life she's known is over and she's not 22 anymore.

My first step to recovery after obtaining a shrink was to cut off any and all contact with my ex (why torture yourself?) and get a lover. Do it. And purchase a Pocket Rocket®. Don't leave home without it. Actually, you may never leave home. Get your pipes cleaned regularly — it really takes a load off, so to speak. This time is about you, and the most important thing you can do for yourself is to take care of yourself. Let's put that in bold type, shall we? . . .

CHAPTER 3

TAKE CARE OF YOURSELF

THE GOAL: Do whatever it takes to feel good about yourself emotionally and physically. Such as…

Eat right.

**If you have a nutty family —
CREATE BOUNDARIES.**

Say "YES" to everything that you think might be fun but that you're too afraid or too lazy to do. Do it, dammit!

Give up being perfect because Christiane Northrup, the famous gyno, says to and because it's true. In fact, rent and read all Northrup all the time. We love her!

P.S. Hate to break it to ya, but you're not perfect anyway. No one is except Daniel Craig.

Be grateful
(not like you live in Bangladesh for cryin' out loud).

RESPECT

Think about what turns you on . . .
Daniel Craig???
Hot air ballooning?
Surfing? Reading?
Just brainstorming here . . .

Embrace stillness.

Be alone. Don't be afraid of it.

Get away and look at nature.

Look hot for YOU.

Hit a fabulous bar and have the perfect cocktail.

Find any goddamn reason to celebrate.

Surround yourself with inspiring, fabulous women who enhance your life.

Dump the toxic ones who bleed you dry.

YOURSELF!

Be kind to yourself.

Fake it till you make it.
It's actually been proven to work —
so, do it.

Embrace change.

Embrace chance.

Get a shrink . . .
a life coach, a trainer, a lover, a whatever . . .
Just get proactive about TAKING CARE OF YOU.

Throw all ideas and dreams at the wall
and see what sticks.

Get strength from a "source"
— books, god, masseuse, nature, vibrator . . .

Create the world you want to live in.
Now is the perfect time to follow your real love,
the real passion in your life — maybe it's not even a man.
A new career?
A new city?
A new pet?
Adopt a mutt!

"It's the friends you can call **AT 4 a.m.** that matter."

– Marlene Dietrich

"The
PRIVILEGE
of a lifetime
is being
who you
are."

— Joseph Campbell

Get Netflix® and rent all you can on Louise Hay . . .
Wayne Dyer, too.
JUST DO IT!

Also — and this is imperative — rent *Rome*.
Because, honestly, you just can't beat porno as
performed by the Royal Shakespeare Company!
It's fabulous! If the Pocket Rocket® doesn't get your juices
flowing, Titus Pullo surely will. Rent *Rome* and use
your Pocket Rocket®. Now that's heaven!

Go with your gut.

De-clutter your life.
Free yourself up from people and stuff. You'll feel light as air.
If you don't love it, CHUCK IT!

If you're dating again — great — good for you!
Don't overanalyze or investigate if the guy doesn't call
you again. You two didn't click. Who cares?
Move on and don't take it personally.
Don't cloud yourself up with negative thoughts.

RAISE YOUR STANDARDS.

We can't reiterate this enough!!!

Practice smiling . . . at everyone!
That is an order!

List all your fears and then turn them into positive statements. On paper.
For example, if you've written, "I'm never going to get over my ex," change it to, "I am so over my ex."

DON'T analyze what you coulda woulda shoulda done.
It's DONE. FINITO! OVER!
Move on.

AND . . .

Don't lean too hard on your friends.
If you're obsessing like crazy get a shrink and reread DUMPED every day. Stop complaining and droning on for crying out loud. We don't want your friends to DUMP YOU, TOO!

Fill your home with love and joy by adding flowers, friends, parties, art, candles, pets...
Paint one wall sexy red just because you wanna!

THE FIRST THING I DID when we broke up was buy an orange couch. He hated that color. It was my "fuck you, it's my house now" sofa.

 I DONATED, SOLD, GAVE AWAY anything and everything I didn't love or need. I want to live simply and feel like I'm in Tahiti or Bermuda at all times. Doesn't everyone?

 **DUMPED BY KING HENRY VIII.** Where were you bitches when I needed you???

Do all the stuff HE didn't want to do.

Stop settling for crumbs!

Plan an exotic trip for yourself...

You don't have to hit "buy" just yet, but fantasize and enjoy thinking of the world beyond your walls. Who knows where it may lead . . .

ENJOY YOUR FREEDOM!

BATHS, BEACHES,

Get over him: Self-care tips

"RED SHOES, BOURBON, AND LOTS AND LOTS OF PIZZA."
HELEN WRIGHT

"Tubs and tubs of chocolate ice cream and lots of porn . . . with a good cigarette."
LEILA BARRATT-DENYER

"I channel that post-breakup anger into fitness and exercise like a maniac. The bonus is I look great in my tight jeans and dresses!"
ANONYMOUS

"Fill your life with music, sweets, beaches, cats . . . If it happens again, I would be sure to have a dog around!"
ANN

"I like to take myself out to a delicious and expensive dinner and remind myself of how fabulous I am."
ANN SCOBIE

"BEING ALONE."
JULIE SALIK-MULQUEEN

AND BOOZE...OH MY!

from brilliant REAL babes

"COOKING DINNER IN CRIMSON LIPSTICK AND STILETTOS PERKS ME UP
INTO ULTRA-FABULOUS MODE – EVEN WHEN INSIDE I'M SO . . . NOT."
LAURA EISMAN, FASHIONISTA

"SOME GREAT UNATTACHED SEX."
JULIE SALIK-MULQUEEN

"My favorite way of taking care of myself is
to travel somewhere new on my own – away from everything
in my regular life that 'defines' me."
MELISSA

"Chick flicks and swathing myself
in soft blankets or pj's."
CHALKLEY CALDERWOOD

"WINE, SUSHI, AND LIFETIME MOVIES."
CHRISTINE

"If my gal pals are available, a giant margarita and guacamole with my peeps.
Otherwise, a nice hot bubble bath with a lovely glass of wine!"
NANCY MEYER

"Taking a good look at myself
naked in the mirror and telling myself,
'I look hot!'"
DANA VANCE

CHAPTER 4

CLOSURE
—HUH?

MJ

I WAS DESPERATE FOR CLOSURE. Desperate. Probably because the breakup blindsided me … or who the hell knows why. The ex and I were already scheduled to go on a Moroccan holiday two weeks after he dumped me. I didn't cancel it. I simply deleted all the romantic spots we were scheduled to hit and went with a gay pal. I was not going to let the ex screw me out of an already-paid-for exotic trip! After a couple of days of camels, sand dunes, and turquoise seas, I began texting the ex like a madwoman begging for some explanation other than the one I got: that he needed to follow his "individual path." I don't even know what the fuck that means …

497 texts later and no response. One afternoon, while alone on a spectacular Moroccan beach, baggy eyed from crying all night and about to send text number 498, it hit me: *HE DIDN'T LOVE ME ANYMORE.* That was the bottom line — and there was nothing I could do about that and nothing he could say to me to make it better. I was tired of crying, tired of begging, tired of not enjoying my exotic vacation.

Save yourself the $749.38 text bill and get over your need for closure. You're never gonna hear what you think you wanna hear.

I DIDN'T HAVE A CLOSURE ISSUE with this last one. We pretty much threw the relationship up in the air and shot it to death. Plus, it's kinda hard to want closure with a guy who doesn't bang ya. *CASE CLOSED*. However, I do remember thinking I needed "closure" when I was in my twenties with the "love of my life." It was pathetic really. I was relentless with the crying and the calling. As time passed, we would get together as "friends" and I'd pray he'd want me back, which, of course, he never did. Finally, after a few of these stupid "just friends" dinners, I begged the guy to tell me he didn't want me and that he didn't love me anymore so that I could move on. He told me he couldn't do that because — ya ready for this one? — "Ya neva know … maybe five or ten years from now we may get back together." What a dick. Granted, he was all of 25 at the time, but he should have known better and been a tad more thoughtful. Yeah, with this last one — the old fart — I looked at him point blank, told him I'd had it, and that I couldn't go on anymore with the way things were. Then I told him: "Grab me, tell me you love me, not to leave you, and that we're gonna make this work." His response: "I can't." Cruel maybe, but boy was I ever grateful.

Closure is ridiculous. And if you're over a certain age, you should know better. Just move on and never look back.

YOU'LL GET "CLOSURE" ALL RIGHT — when you and you alone have found your joy again. You will find this "closure" bullshit when you have forgiven yourself and your ex and are taking care of yourself. Taking care of yourself and smiling as you walk down the street in your tight jeans, fuck-me pumps, and bright red lipstick!

We never ever want to hear you utter that blasphemous word "closure" again. Got it? Enough! **IT'S BULLSHIT.** If you are waiting to have closure with your ex at some secluded restaurant where he tells you shit you've been imagining you want him to tell you about your relationship and why it ended blah blah blah … fuck it. This person you want to have your special talk (aka "closure") with is scratching his balls sittin' on his disgusting couch, watching football, and could give two shits about your closure plan.

Sooooooo therefore … Cut off, cut off, cut off!!! It's not about *him* anymore. For now, what is most important is *YOU*. So, don't talk to him. We're not saying forever, but not for a mighty good long time. Like until you're healthy, happy, married, remarried, moved to Paris, forgotten his birthday, forgotten his name, and are retired and living in a nursing home with your mouth hanging wide open at all times … then — and only then — you may, by all means, give him a call.

DO NOT UNDER ANY CIRCUMSTANCES
have breakup sex with your ex...

THAT'S WHAT WHORES ARE FOR!!

Be decisive.

Risk.

Self-care.

Enjoy today.

Be conscious of your thoughts and what you say.

Believe in yourself.

This is going to be the best year yet.

This is going to be the best decade yet.

Tune out complainers.

If you're not getting much joy with your current guy — whatcha waiting for? An invitation?

Get the hell out!

Stop mourning the fantasy of who you wish he was and get a grip on the pathetic reality of who he will always be.
– Jane Gennaro

Storage space: $45 a month.

One-way ticket out of town: $169.95

The freedom to move out of your boyfriend's apartment without a dime in your pocket: Priceless. – Vickie Schmitt

I traded in my husband for a dog, who's loyal and doesn't snore.
– Alex Forman

I never lose sight of the fact that just being is fun.
– Kate Hepburn wannabe friend

So, after 25 years he left me for another woman. But I'll be okay. I've got my health and I know that someday there'll be a guy in the nursing home who's gonna think I'm smokin' hot!
– Cynthia Grow

Thank you for breaking my heart... you've made me stronger.
– Anonymous

Honestly, after my breakups, I need a lot of male attention. Last time, I joined the old men's Game Club at Posto 6 in Copacabana, in the hopes that I'd learn to play chess. But, I had to leave my membership when the 86-year-old and 78-year-old got into a fist fight over who was going to teach me a move. – Alex Forman

This helped me: I took his picture, ripped it up, put it in the toilet, peed on it, and flushed it.
– Jennifer Jiles ex-Rockette

Be Brave!
– SunHee Grinnell

No more drunk emailing. Write to your heart's content – but don't you dare hit Send!! – Pamela Fahey

Listen to the voice that speaks to you when you lay your head on the pillow at night. You know you're better off.
– Leila Barratt-Denyer

Twenty years from now you will be more disappointed by the things that you didn't do than by the ones you did do.
– Mark Twain wannabe friend

Screw him – rather, don't – and move on!
– Nancy Meyer

Delete his number and get yourself a new one.
– Jane H.

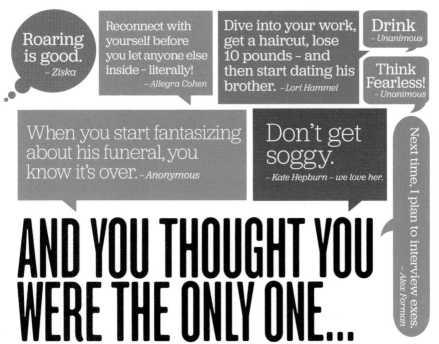

Roaring is good. – *Ziska*

Reconnect with yourself before you let anyone else inside – literally! – *Allegra Cohen*

Dive into your work, get a haircut, lose 10 pounds – and then start dating his brother. – *Lori Hammel*

Drink – *Unanimous*

Think Fearless! – *Unanimous*

When you start fantasizing about his funeral, you know it's over. – *Anonymous*

Don't get soggy. – *Kate Hepburn – we love her.*

Next time, I plan to interview exes. – *Alex Forman*

AND YOU THOUGHT YOU WERE THE ONLY ONE...

Advice from some of our fabulous friends...

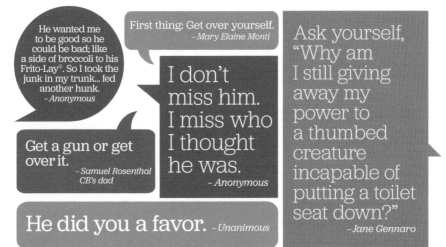

He wanted me to be good so he could be bad; like a side of broccoli to his Frito-Lay®. So I took the junk in my trunk... fed another hunk. – *Anonymous*

First thing: Get over yourself. – *Mary Elaine Monti*

I don't miss him. I miss who I thought he was. – *Anonymous*

Ask yourself, "Why am I still giving away my power to a thumbed creature incapable of putting a toilet seat down?" – *Jane Gennaro*

Get a gun or get over it. – *Samuel Rosenthal CB's dad*

He did you a favor. – *Unanimous*

"I'm a woman of very few words but lots of **ACTION**."

– Mae West

Be a lot of woman!
Weed out the wusses who are intimidated.
Screw anyone who has a problem with you
being a lot of girl!

Not having sex anymore?
Get out! It's OVER!
That ship has sailed.
That pie is burnt.
That cow has been put out to pasture.

IT'S
OVER.

CHAPTER 5

RED
FLAGS

RED FLAGS WITH MY EX? Well, let's just say he used to buy two of everything when he loved something. Curious . . . one for "our" house and one for . . . uhh . . . his single future perhaps? Duh!

THE BIG RED FLAG WITH MY EX was that he couldn't compliment me. Couldn't tell me I was attractive every once in a while. The old dude just couldn't muster the words. He'd tell everyone else how he felt about me, *except me.* And you know what? Begging for a compliment is bullshit. Geez . . . tell a girl she's beautiful! It's not rocket science and you may even get a blow job out of it.

MJ

I KEPT BEGGING MY MAN to shave his scratchy beard, which looked like shit, so we could have *real* makeout sessions again. I'd also tease him about a sexy man I worked with and how I'd love to "do" him. Ex's response: "I just want you happy, so DO him if you wanna." What a prince!

Scaring him when you wear garters?

Does he find your sexy lingerie "too much"?

Does he shy away from a good pounding?

How you say in English? ... **HE GAY**??

CUT YOUR LOSSES, LADIES, AND GET OUT!

DUE TO MY SEX-STARVED relationship, when my doctor put his big gnarly sexy palm on my belly, I could have orgasmed right then and there. Pathetic!

ON OUR LAST SEXLESS, unromantic vacation, my ex pulled me over to check out some earrings he was looking at in a store. Did I like them? I thought, my word, what's gotten into him? I might actually blow this guy tonight! Of course, I thought he was thinking of buying the earrings for *me*. Wrong.

On our "romantic" getaway trip he's shopping for his grown daughter. Sexy! Not only did I not blow him, I dumped him a month later.

"Good sex is like good bridge. If you don't have a **GOOD PARTNER** you better have a **GOOD HAND**."

– Mae West

POP QUIZ #1: DUH...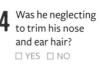

1 Was he buying presents for the other women in his life — like his secretary, kid, or mother — and not you?
□ YES □ NO

2 Was it hard to get a hold of him when he was away on business trips?
□ YES □ NO

2b Were you getting sporadic texts at odd times when he was away on these business trips?
□ YES □ NO

3 Were his holiday/birthday presents getting really pathetic like wine glasses or a pedometer?
□ YES □ NO

4 Was he neglecting to trim his nose and ear hair?
□ YES □ NO

5 Did he take a dump with the door open?
□ YES □ NO

5b Did YOU?
□ YES □ NO

6 Were you begging to be kissed?
□ YES □ NO

7 Were you begging for him to tell you he loved you?
□ YES □ NO

8 Did his eyes roll to the back of his head when you tried to "communicate"?
□ YES □ NO

9 Did he stop including you when he went out with his friends?
□ YES □ NO

10 Was he unenthusiastic about everything where you were concerned?
□ YES □ NO

11 Was he moody as all hell?
□ YES □ NO

11b Were YOU?
□ YES □ NO

12 Were you having a lot less fun with him?
□ YES □ NO

13 Did you keep writing in your journal . . . "Am I happy with

_____
(fill in the asshole's name)
yet"?
□ YES □ NO

What were you thinking???

14 Was he paying more attention to your girlfriends than to you when you went out?
☐ YES ☐ NO

15 Did it take eons for him to get a hard on?
☐ YES ☐ NO

15b How 'bout YOU?
☐ YES ☐ NO

16 Was he avoiding sex?
☐ YES ☐ NO

16b Were YOU?
☐ YES ☐ NO

17 Were you shutting up more and more to "keep the peace"?
☐ YES ☐ NO

18 Plain and simple: Did he adore you?
☐ YES ☐ NO

18b . . . And vice versa?
☐ YES ☐ NO

19 Was he more passionate about his motorcycle then he was about YOU??
☐ YES ☐ NO

20 Did you feel less sexy and less confident more often?
☐ YES ☐ NO

21 Did you go dutch on your birthday? (This has seriously occurred!)
☐ YES ☐ NO

(If you answer **YES** to this, your assignment is to reread DUMPED 10 times.)

22 Did he gain 30 pounds?
☐ YES ☐ NO

22b Did YOU?
☐ YES ☐ NO

23 Were you staying in your relationship for the sole reason that you were afraid to be alone?
☐ YES ☐ NO

Ladies, if you answered **YES** more than 12 times, you were **SCREWED** and not in the good way. Praise the lord, you got the hell out of that **BULLSHIT** relationship!

YOU'D BE AMAZED at how many of your friends in relationships are not having sex … they don't have the balls to leave or are too lazy to change it up. But, they ain't as happy as they want you to think they are. No fucky, no happy.

DON'T BE A PARANOID NUT, but pay attention. Don't settle for crumbs. You deserve the best. If he's buying earrings for his daughter, he better damn well be buying you something fabulous and going down on you to boot!

"Life is either a daring **ADVENTURE** or nothing at all."

– *Helen frickin' Keller*

It's **NOT OKAY** to be dumped on.

NOT OKAY to not be there for your partner.

NOT OKAY to be ignored.

You are not invisible.

You are to be **ADORED!**

That's the word for the day. And for life – **ADORED!**

SMART CHICKS TELL HOW

Eventually

"Red flags?
You mean like not hearing
from him for days,
women calling the house,
cocaine nosebleeds,
and booty calls at 2 a.m.?"
DANA VANCE

"WHEN MY EX-LOVER REQUESTED THAT I WAX THE HAIR ON MY KNUCKLES."
LEILA BARRATT-DENYER

"When my 36-year-old boyfriend confessed to me
that I was his first 'relationship' since high school.
Wow, what was I thinking?"
MJ

"WHEN A GUY SAYS NO WOMAN HAS EVER UNDERSTOOD HIS INDEPENDENT SPIRIT."
ANN SCOBIE

"LET'S SEE:
**there was the fact that he had had shock therapy
and was on a cocktail of no less than 12 meds…"**
CHALKLEY CALDERWOOD

TO SPOT A RED FLAG...

anyway...

"HIS DOG'S NAME WAS 'MAME'"

ANDREA BIANCHI

"An ex once told me that he could lie on top of his old girlfriend when they were both fully clothed and she'd orgasm. Like magic, I guess…"

CB

"How about no sex, insane hours in front of the TV, longer trips to the 'golf house,' and not caring if I joined him or not?"

ANNA STUART

"HE STOPPED WANTING TO HAVE SEX, SAYING HE WAS JUST TIRED. ALL THE TIME. I ACTUALLY BELIEVED IT AND FELT BAD FOR HIM!"

ANONYMOUS

"There were so many red flags I thought I was in a ceremonial Chinese parade …"

LEILA BARRATT-DENYER

"WHEN I FIRST MET MY HUSBAND I THOUGHT HE WAS GAY … NEED I SAY MORE?"

ANONYMOUS

CHAPTER 6

LET IT GO

I TACKLED ONE OF MY GREATEST FEARS of being alone by going to the country solo for six weeks. I used that time to take on yoga and meditation — two things I never thought I'd be into and now love. I read the classics, enjoyed nature, and cooked healthily. I embraced the solitude even when it was tough. It was the best thing I could have done for myself. I came back charged, creative, and centered. I worship my alone time now. I confronted my worst fear and things turned out pretty damn great.

I WAS USED TO LEAVING TOWN on the weekends for ten years. Lovely to have a getaway place but not at the expense of keeping a dying relationship going. Anyhow, something drew me to a small town on the water, and I started going on day trips there with my dog. It really helped me to clear my head. I find that silence and nature nurture the soul and allow your thoughts to become focused and clear. Then, of course, I have a cocktail at a fabulous place on the water. It has been the best medicine for me in my recovery.

AS YOU FACE YOUR FEARS, ask yourself, "What's the worst possible thing that could happen to me?" Prison? Well, that's not gonna happen! So, get over it! Things will never be as bad as you've imagined.

Of course, Anne Boleyn faced her worst fears and . . . well, who coulda predicted that one??

"It's **NEVER TOO LATE** to be what you might have been."

– *George Eliot*

"The foolish ~~man~~ woman seeks **HAPPINESS** in the distance, the wise ~~man~~ woman grows it under ~~his~~ her feet."

– James Oppenheim

"TIME HEALS" as the saying goes. We're speeding up the process.

Do yoga. ✳

Regret nothing.

DING DING DING (this is huge):
Forgive yourself and your ex so you can move on.
It's a bitch, but do it for yourself, not him.
Duh! We don't give a crap about him. We like YOU!

✳ For all you advanced chicks:
Try chanting and be sure to let us
know how it goes. We may be too
busy getting drunk on our perfect
cocktails, but we'd love to hear!

Always remember that your ex did you a favor.

Be grateful for that time in your life, forgive the asshole, and …

PUT IT DOWN.

LISTEN, I LOVED MY EX. I wouldn't have spent 10 years with him if I didn't. We met for a reason, stayed for a season, and thought we'd be together for a lifetime. Two outta three ain't bad. It ran its course or . . . who cares why anymore? I'm grateful he was in my life and I'm grateful it's over. I'm grateful I never have to see his brother's balls again. I want him to be happy — not flourish, you understand, just happy. (Who is this evolved person?? I don't even recognize myself!)

WELL, IT TOOK ME A YEAR to wish my ex well. Now, I'm able to say that I'm grateful for the six out of seven great years we had together. I no longer feel the need for "closure" over dinner, sex for old time's sake, or any other crap. I feel liberated and ready for my next adventure.

CHAPTER 7

BE
OPEN

THIS IS SERIOUSLY CORNY, BUT . . . Look in the mirror every day and say "I love you." As awkward as that may seem to you, it's good to do. Eventually, you'll mean what you say and you'll realize loving yourself is huge — not just in recovering from a breakup but in dealing with every aspect of your life.

DON'T WORRY ABOUT "BEING COOL." Try new things. You may be a "dork" sometimes, but do you really care what people think at this point in the game? Impress yourself. Look fabulous for YOU. Even when you walk the dog. Ditch your ugly ripped sweats. There are sexy ones out there. Besides, Oprah wouldn't approve, and who doesn't obey Oprah?

Salsa!

Karaoke!

Date — just for the fun of it: PRACTICE, PRACTICE, PRACTICE.

Get out. Be a barfly for a night.

Go horseback riding!
(It might just get your cooch going!)

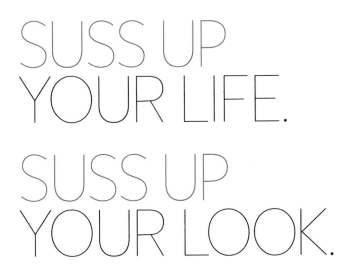

SUSS UP
YOUR LIFE.

SUSS UP
YOUR LOOK.

Visualize **WHAT** you want – not just **WHO** you want – in your life.

IMAGINE
A LIFE
OF
POSSIBILITIES...

Do everything your ex never wanted to do, like exploring an exotic country.

Recite affirmations and express gratitude every morning and every night.

Live in abundance — you deserve it.

VOLUNTEER.
GIVE BACK.
It will come back to you in spades!!!!!!

"Travel light.
Live light.
Spread
the light.
BE THE LIGHT."

– Yogi Bhajan

(We found this on a frickin' tea bag!)

CB

IF YOU TOLD ME TWO YEARS AGO I would be seeing a new-agey shrink and actually loving her, I would have done a spit take, but it so happens that working with her has been fantastic. I never bike ride, but I was open to it one afternoon with MJ on Governor's Island and I had a helluva time. Of course, we rode around in search of a killer bar — excellent destination — faster on bike than foot. The point is, I started saying "YES" to new ideas.

I may be opinionated on a lot of topics (in case you couldn't tell), but I'm also a lot more open these days . . . baby steps, but it's a start.

MJ

I'M A LIST MAKER . . . AND A PROCRASTINATOR.
I had a list of all the stuff I wanted to do
"when I had the time." After he dumped me,
I had a whole lot of time. I never thought I'd
become one of those women who meditates
and does daily affirmations at daybreak.
And yet, after being open to CB's suggestion
of reading Louise Hay, Wayne Dyer, and
a dash of Eckhart Tolle, I'm up bright and
early and loving my quiet time. I'm even a
health nut now, and my fridge is no longer
a storage vault for vodka and takeout food.
It's amazing how change begets change.
I've also created a home studio to work on
personal projects. I wasn't sure that would
suit me but I went with it. I didn't doubt
myself, and turns out I'm loving it!

"Things do not change. **WE CHANGE.**"

– Henry David Thoreau

Sometimes, we stick with the familiar because it's easy. Let that go, girls!

RISK!
Liberate yourself from old habits!

CHAPTER 8

YOU DESERVE A SEX LIFE

I HAVE TO SAY that sexual power ruled me as a young woman. Now, I'm searching for a more meaningful power. A power that will serve me for a lifetime. Before my last relationship I did just about everybody in town. I desperately needed some time off from the sex thing — especially coming off the last one with his lousy libido. I say, take some time off from sex if you feel like it and then come back to it.

CB

NOT TOO MUCH TIME, THOUGH, because the longer you live without it, the longer you can go without it. Plus, you gotta "use it or lose it" as the gynecological saying goes! If you ladies have gone too long without doing it and are fearful, do not fret!!!! Practice with a zucchini and a Pocket Rocket® to start. Add lots of KY® and Astroglide® and voilá! You'll have a fabulous recipe for sex! Then, you'll graduate to the real deal and bask in the glow of a kick-ass orgasm!

IF YOU'RE GUN SHY REGARDING SEX, just get over it. WILL yourself to fuck. Fake it till you make it — this shit works. Your sex drive is mental. Use your imagination. Fantasize. Get that brain of yours horny again. Read trashy novels, read porn, watch porn, think of Daniel Craig … Do whatever is necessary to turn yourself on! Lose weight, do Kegel exercises, eat oysters, wear crotchless panties, and diddle yourself! Hope we're freaking out all you evangelicals out there.

"Take your **PLEASURE** seriously."

— *Charles Eames*

YOU DESERVE A **SEX** LIFE...

Make this your MANTRA.

CHAPTER 9

TURNING
POINTS

CB

A YEAR BEFORE MY BREAKUP a friend had recommended the book *Skinny Bitch*, for my burger/wing/vodka addiction, not for weight loss. What hit home for me was taking care of myself by thinking about what I eat, being kinder to the planet, and dumping the toxic people in my life. (Uh, who are you and what have you done with the real Caryn??) A few weeks after finishing *Skinny Bitch*, I dumped my ex. Also dumped burgers and wings. Will never dump my vodka. **NEVER.** (Now I recognize you!)

AFTER I WAS DUMPED FLAT ON MY ASS and my worst fear was realized, I was strangely exhilarated. Deep down I had wanted him to do it. I probably even drove him to it, because I knew I was better off without him. I just didn't have the balls to end it myself. God love him — the prick set me free. In time, I got my sense of self back. My joy. My dignity. My confidence. Oh, and I don't have to pretend his big belly is cute anymore.

DUMPED

THE BOOK

IS YOUR TURNING POINT!

TURNING POINTS

You're in good company

"IT'S ALL ABOUT TIME."

ANNETTA MARION

"I knew I was going to be okay
when I realized I didn't love him anymore.
That, in fact, I never really did love him.
I was addicted to the drama."
MYRA KLOCKENBRINK

"Rather than get annoyed
when the construction workers
hooted and whistled at me,
I smiled and thought,
'Yeah! I do look good
and I'm back in the game.'"

ANONYMOUS

"When I only thought of him once a week
instead of seven times a day."
CHALKLEY CALDERWOOD

WE REALLY LOVE!

with these real women.

"I remember saying out loud
that I am going to be OKAY.
I am going to be OKAY.
I put that OKAY sign up on my fridge,
on my doors – everywhere –
and eventually,

I FELT IT!"

LEILA BARRATT-DENYER

"I THINK MY EPIPHANY CAME
WHEN I REALIZED THAT
THERE WERE THINGS IN A RELATIONSHIP
THAT I HAD ALWAYS DREAMED OF
AND THAT THERE WAS SOMEONE OUT THERE
WITH WHOM I COULD HAVE
ALL THOSE THINGS
AND MORE."
HELEN WRIGHT

"WHEN I FELT EXCITED ABOUT LIFE AGAIN."

CHALKLEY CALDERWOOD

CHAPTER 10

HELLO, GORGEOUS

(yeah, *you*...)

GETTING OLDER? Well, hallelujah! Good for you! It's about time! You're getting wiser. Putting up with a lot less shit. Owning your own shit. Gaining confidence.

Look in that mirror every day and tell yourself, "I love you!" Love your laugh lines, you sexy thang, and love what you see. You are hot. Not just on the outside, doll, but on the inside, too.

By taking care of yourself you gain confidence and self-esteem.

AND THAT IS GREAT BEAUTY!

You are hot when you are filled with...

JOY & BLISS

BUYING STUFF WILL NOT FILL YOUR SOUL. A little retail therapy once in a while is fun. Just get yourself one thing that makes you feel sexy again. A new lipstick, a jaunty hat, a push-up bra, those crotchless panties you've had your eye on …

IF YOUR EX DUMPED YOU FOR SOMEBODY YOUNGER … fuck him and his tiny pecker. Just forgive the ass (we'll hate the stupid motherfucker for ya), move on, and find yourself a nice big stud. And be grateful you're not 22 and clueless about how to give a proper blow job.

"If you obey all the rules, you miss **ALL THE FUN**."

– *Katharine Hepburn*

I CELEBRATE MYSELF much more as I get older. I'm feeling beautiful and sexy in whatever I'm wearing or not wearing. I don't pay much attention to the rules of fashion and I only dress for me. I'm loving my newly blonde bangs and brand-spankin'-new hot pleather pants! When I see old pictures from the last two years with my ex, I can't get over how frumpy and grumpy I looked. And felt. No sex'll do that to you every time. Love yourself and do joyful things and you will glow from the inside out!

CB

GOD, I FELT OLD. Old and unsexy and washed up really. Once I walked away from what was keeping me down — the ex — I lost 205 pounds — 200 of him and 5 of me! Then I began working on my head and keeping it together by being open and curious and joyful. How? By doing what I wanted to do and getting out and doing fun things! That is sexy. Fun is sexy! I don't question putting on a pair of stilettos with a short skirt if I want to. Screw the fashionistas! I'm enjoying taking care of myself and finding out more about what turns me on . . . in and out of the bedroom. And most days I think I'm pretty dang good lookin'!

Go blonde for kicks.
Go against the rules.
Wear red lipstick
and nothing else.
Let your hair grow out
and be long at any age!
Work a mini
if you want to.

FUCK THE RULES!

Enjoy being you.

Explore who you really are and what you really like.

"The maxim 'nothing but **PERFECTION**' may be spelled **PARALYSIS**."

– *Winston Churchill*

Love your body no matter what age you are.
Take care and love your body, and it will love you back.

Get into a hot soapy bath with a glass of wine or a fabulous martini and luxuriate.
There are water-resistant vibrators, FYI... or there's the faucet. Just sayin'!

Visualize your sexy self.
Wanna wear some pleather and ride around on a moped in Paris for a few months?

DO IT!

EVER NOTICE HOW SOCIETY NEVER DISCUSSES SAGGY BALLS? Hmmmm...

SUPPLEMENT

Lucky you. All our hard work in a nutshell

FILMS

THE DEEP ONES

Cléo from 5 to 7
Foreign but worth it!

Klute
Jane plays the greatest whore

THE PICK-ME-UPS

Auntie Mame
We wanna be Rosalind Russell. Oh we are

Baby Boom
Talk about reinventing yourself

Superbad
Just for laughs

The First Wives Club
Revenge is so sweet

Bridget Jones's Diary
She's all of us

Legally Blonde
Never underestimate yourself

THE TAWDRY DUO

Rome
Pocket Rocket® in hand . . .

The Tudors
Replace batteries

BOOKS

THE DEEP ONE

Broken Open
by Elizabeth Lesser

THE INSPIRATIONS

When Things Fall Apart
by Pema Chödrön

Skinny Bitch
by Rory Freedman and Kim Barnouin

My Life So Far
by Jane Fonda

On Becoming Fearless . . .
in Love, Work, and Life
by Arianna Huffington

A New Earth
by Eckart Tolle

Just Kids
by Patti Smith

Atlas Shrugged
by Ayn Rand

THE PICK-ME-UPS

The Principles of Uncertainty
by Maira Kalman

Bridget Jones's Diary
by Helen Fielding

THIS...

— the best of the best!

DVDS

THE INSPIRATIONS

You Can Heal Your Life

Receiving Prosperity

Dissolving Barriers
All by Louise Hay

Mother-Daughter Wisdom
Dr. Christiane Northrup

There's a Spiritual Solution to Every Problem
Wayne Dyer

THE TANTALIZING

Viva la Vulva
*Betty Dodson,
the mother of masturbation*

THE PICK-ME-UP

Sex & the City
*Anything from the first
two years of the series*

AND THE SONGS...

THE KICK-ASS

I Will Survive
by Gloria Gaynor (It's the anthem after all!)

"F**k You!"
by Cee-lo Green

You're Breaking My Heart
by Harry Nilsson

Did I Shave My Legs for This?
by Deana Carter

I Can See Clearly Now
by Johnny Nash

Joy
by Lucinda Williams

I'm Looking Through You
by The Beatles

I'm Coming Out
by Diana Ross

Songs for the Dumped
by Ben Folds Five

50 Ways to Leave Your Lover
by Paul Simon

OKAY, OKAY, JUST ONE MORE...

Heartbreaker
by Pat Benatar

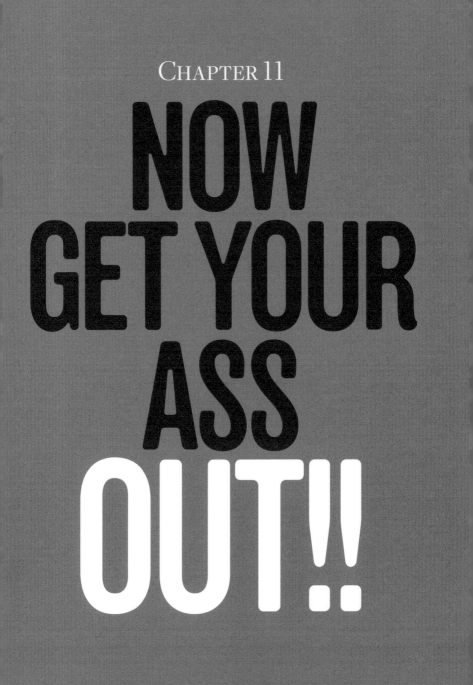

CHAPTER 11

NOW GET YOUR ASS OUT!!

GO OUT. GO OUT.
GO OUT!

Sit at a restaurant bar alone or with friends and own it.

WE'RE NOT SAYING hunt down a new love.

WE'RE SAYING LIVE, meet people, and most important, have fun!

Tick tock, gals ...
And we ain't talkin'
about biological
clocks here. We are
talking about life.

I TRY TO DO ONE NEW THING A DAY in my hometown. It might be as simple as using the gorgeous reading room at the New York Public Library or exploring a different part of the city on my bike or maybe nursing a cocktail at a much-ballyhooed lounge. It's fun to view your city as a tourist sees it, with fresh eyes! I've also spent extended periods of time exploring other cultures — the more remote, the better for me. I've always loved traveling, and now I'm free to commit to two months at a time in exotic locales, which is something I've wanted to do for years. Of course, I do have bills to pay. I just schedule my life carefully and in advance. Not having to coordinate with a significant other has freed me, and I'm taking advantage of it. Last year, I went to Southeast Asia. This year ... who knows? My advice to you is to follow your gut and see the world or just rediscover your own town. Be curious!!

I HELD MYSELF BACK FROM TAKING VACATIONS because I was always afraid I'd miss out on a job. Screw that! I now seize multiple opportunities to go sit on a beach in North Florida! I get to wake up to the sunrise and crashing waves and hang out with folks who never use their cell phones unless it's an emergency — heaven. I come back home to NYC recharged and excited to work, see shows, and hang with friends. Sure, I could hole myself up in my apartment with my two-legged dog, surf the computer, order in, and watch Bravo — all great — but I know that I have to make an effort to get out!!!! We're all too fabulous to be shut-ins.

"If you want to see the girl next door, **GO NEXT DOOR**."

- Joan Crawford

BE YOUR OWN ADVOCATE.

Tell your friends and even strangers along the way, "Hey, if you know any nice people … I'm dating again." Be bold. It's a numbers game. You might meet ten people and maybe you'll only like one, and guess what? That's great! You're out there meeting new people, whether it's a lover, a friend, or someone you'll write about someday because he was so god-awful you just had to put pen to paper. Hmmmm…we smell a sitcom!

Be spiritual. But don't lose your sense of humor, for god's sake.

Do joyful and fun things. It's an example of loving yourself — and kinda spiritual, too.

Ride a bike in a beautiful setting.
Open up to joy and nature.
Notice the little things.

Hang with joyful, positive, fun people.
Dump those complicated, joyless friends of yours.
They will drain the living shit out of you.
They aren't even your frickin' family members, so —

DUMP
THEM NOW.

It's pure and simple —
good friends
enhance your world.

"Everything
in life
is based
on
DARING."
– *Martin Buber*

IT'S EASY to fall back on what's familiar. Risk takes balls.

CHALLENGE YOURSELF.

It will be the most rewarding and proudest moment of your life.

STEP OUT OF YOUR COMFORT ZONE!

LADIES, LET THE

Think beyond your four walls
and travel! That's right — go it alone

SPLURGE

Butterfield & Robinson

Bike from winery to winery in Bordeaux or gelateria to gelateria in Tuscany, or dozens of other destinations around the world! Booze and ice cream… Where do we sign up?!
butterfield.com

COMO Shambhala Estate, Bali

This over-the-top-luxurious wellness retreat in the rain forest is a world leader in pampering, from massage to butler-serviced villas. We're saving up for this one!
cse.como.bz

Country Walkers

From the Tour du Mont Blanc to New Zealand — sign up for these small-group adventures. Sounds exotic — we likey!
countrywalkers.com

AVERAGE PRICED

Mountain Lodges of Peru

Inca Trail treks, nights in stylish lodges staffed with chefs and massage therapists. Heaven!
mountainlodgesofperu.com

Off-the-Beaten Path, Western USA

Watch whales, climb high peaks, raft down rapids, and soak up Southwestern spirituality. Ommmmmm…
offthebeatenpath.com

Rancho La Puerta, Mexico

A week's worth of nature, hiking, and homegrown organic food at this destination spa. And tequila!
rancholapuerta.com

ADVENTURES BEGIN...

We've found some small-group travel options
that attract other solo travelers …
ya never know who you might meet — just saying!

CHEAPISH

Bikini Boot Camp, Mexico

A healthy week of beach walks, workouts, and yoga. Don't worry — there are cocktails aplenty, too.
bikinibootcamp.com

Soukya, India

Detox at one of India's premier Ayurvedic centers in Bangalore. We'll be thinking about you. Go to DUMPED411.com and let us know how it goes!
soukya.com

The Island Experience, Brazil

Seven blissful days of rain forest hiking, sea kayaking, snorkeling, yoga, meditation, massage, beach, and yummy Brazilian eye candy.
theislandexperience.com

DIRT CHEAP

These packages range from assisted backpacking with a guide to a tad more plush. Taxi!
tucantravel.com
intrepidtravel.com
gadventures.com

EVEN CHEAPER THAN DIRT

TRAVEL + VOLUNTEERISM = FREE

Turtle Teams, Worldwide

Join one of thousands of organizations that help threatened sea turtles. CB has saved a few in her hometown!
seaturtles.org
cccturtle.org

Conservation Volunteers, Australia & New Zealand

Work in teams to protect habitats and promote ecotourism. Those Aussie and New Zealand peeps are pretty dang good lookin', FYI …
conservationvolunteers.com.au

Appalachian Trail Conference, USA

This classic long trail in the eastern U.S. is home to almost 2,000 endangered species. Volunteers help with trail building and maintenance. You'll feel great about yourself when you're doing something great for the environment!!
appalachiantrail.org

OR…

Switch apartments or houses with somebody who lives in a fabulous place! Why not?!
homexchangevacation.com

CHAPTER 12

RELAPSES

(suck)

YOU ARE GOING TO RELAPSE. Birthdays and anniversaries are milestones that may lead to reflection and sadness. When you find out he's seeing someone new … that's a big milestone. When you get upset, remind yourself to be grateful for all that you have. Be grateful you're not with him anymore — that you don't have to put up with his gross habits (like spitting and farting) or his all-around bullshit anymore. It's not like your ex has miraculously changed. He's not a better person/lover/friend to someone else. Get that crap out of your head. He's not going to get better with time like a frickin' wine. He is who he is for life. You think he's working on himself? Seriously? Who gives a shit anyway?! It's about you. So, head for those perfect cocktails wearing your fuck-mes and red lipstick and have a party because you are …

FREE!
FREE!
FREE!!

"Let FREE

DOM ring"

— *Samuel Francis Smith*

MJ

THAT FIRST HOLIDAY SEASON was a bitch for me. I was sad and alone in my apartment obsessing over what he was doing that very same moment. Who did he bring to his family's house *this* year? Is he thinking of all the holidays *we* spent together there? I found myself longing for the routine of it all. I missed being a couple.

The holidays fuck everyone up! I was on the brink of reaching out to my ex when I called my oldest and best girlfriend instead. She's a very wise French woman. She patiently listened to me drone on. When I was done, she asked if he'd reached out to me even once since dumping me. Clearly, the answer was a resounding *NO!* She reminded me that he hadn't been there for me for a long time and added that he became a big fat "peeeeeg" (that's French for pig) by the end of our time together anyway. That snapped me out of my funk 'cause it was all true.

I began to remember him and those family times more clearly. Between running around trying to keep him out of the liquor cabinet and off his mother's lap, I was exhausted. It was nostalgia, surrounded by holiday craziness, that had lured me back and made it something it was not. Try not to idealize the person and the times you had. Accept that you will do this anyway, but know that it will lessen over time.

CB

SO I'M OUT WITH AN OLD FRIEND I hadn't seen in years … gay pal. I tell him the big news that I'm no longer with the ex and get zero reaction. Seems he already knew, having seen my ex with another woman only two weeks prior. In the Hamptons no less, which means the ex and said new woman were staying in a hotel … yada yada. You can imagine how my wheels were spinning. After my friend dropped this bomb on me I coasted through dinner, got home, and lost it. I was an absolute mess. We'd only been broken up for three months, for god's sake! The thoughts racing through my mind included "Like he's really gonna find someone better than me?" "I was the best thing that ever happened to that jerk" and "Seriously??" The next morning I knew I had to get my shit together. I thought of all that I'm grateful for, including that I'm not with the ex anymore, and I kept coming up with more stuff to be thankful for. I talked myself off a ledge in less than 24 hours, which was impressive for me.

Think of your relapses like Weight Watchers.® You're on track with your new way of life and one day you pig out. But you don't beat yourself up because you get to start fresh again the next day. Three steps forward, one step back, and so on. Life happens. Relapses happen. Friends drop bombs. People blow diets. As a very wise woman once said, "Tomorrow is another day." That'd be Scarlett. *O'Hara.*

If you can laugh, you can live. Nobody owes you anything. Choose to **BE HAPPY.**

VERY IMPORTANT:

DO NOT BEAT YOURSELF UP!!

You're going to relapse.
You're only human.
You will have bad days.
Tomorrow is a new day.

"Don't look back.
Neurotics
live in
the past.
LIVE IN TODAY.
Enjoy the
journey!"

– Samuel Rosenthal

CB's dad

POP QUIZ #2: FEELING

1 Did you dump his shit at Goodwill?
☐ YES ☐ NO

2 Are you getting your ass off the couch and into the gym?
☐ YES ☐ NO

3 Are you meditating or just taking some quiet time for yourself?
☐ YES ☐ NO

4 Have you tried looking in the mirror each day and saying, "Girl, I friggin' love you?"
☐ YES ☐ NO

5 Are you having good sex — with a partner or with yourself?
☐ YES ☐ NO

6 Are you smiling at everyone as you walk down the street?
☐ YES ☐ NO

7 Did you have a vegetable today?
☐ YES ☐ NO

8 Are you waxing, shaving, and plucking in preparation for some hot last-minute sex with your neighbor, boy toy, lover, date, self?
☐ YES ☐ NO

9 Are you getting at least seven hours of sleep?
☐ YES ☐ NO

10 Have you bought yourself some sexy/naughty lingerie?
☐ YES ☐ NO

11 Have you ordered up ROME or THE TUDORS from Netflix® yet?
☐ YES ☐ NO

12 Did you purchase your Pocket Rocket®?
☐ YES ☐ NO

13 Are you taking advantage of your alone time by doing a face mask while relaxing in a hot tub with a glass of wine?
☐ YES ☐ NO

14 Have you dumped your toxic friends and created boundaries with obnoxious family members?
☐ YES ☐ NO

15 Have you cleared the clutter in your home? (When you clear your clutter, you clear your mind!!!)
☐ YES ☐ NO

FAB YET?

Let's just see about that...

16 Are you reaching out to your fabulous, positive, supportive women friends, aka drinking buddies?
☐ YES ☐ NO

17 Are you visualizing what you want out of this next chapter of your life? (Career, love, travel ... whatever! Use your imagination and let it soar!!)
☐ YES ☐ NO

18 Did you call a shrink if you felt you needed it? (Remember — it's like a massage!)
☐ YES ☐ NO

19 Speaking of ... Have you scheduled a massage or manicure to pamper yourself?
☐ YES ☐ NO

20 Have you sat at a bar solo looking hot as hell? Even for one drink?? Baby steps ...
☐ YES ☐ NO

21 Have you eased up on your regrets bullshit?
☐ YES ☐ NO

22 Have you burned his love letters or at least most of them?
☐ YES ☐ NO

23 Are you resisting the urge to email, phone, or text him?
☐ YES ☐ NO

24 Have you said your affirmations today?
☐ YES ☐ NO

25 Have you said "yes" more often than "no"?
☐ YES ☐ NO

TOTALS

YES _____ NO _____

If you marked **16** Yeses, you go girl!!!!

If you marked **20** Nos, consider yourself bitch-slapped and repeat the quiz in a week! Promise yourself that you will make an effort and take the risk!!!

CHAPTER 13

THAT JOY THANG

THIS MAY SOUND CLICHÉ, BUT I DON'T GIVE A SHIT.
I've gone and created the life I've been fantasizing about for years. I work less for my clients and more for myself, creating projects I believe in. When I'm not working or enjoying my neighborhood, I go for extensive vacations in exotic places I never thought I'd go to. When I meet that sexy, hung grown-up with a huge joie de vivre, I'm ready and open!

I'M LEADING A MORE STRESS-FREE EXISTENCE,
considering a country retreat and contemplating doing yoga rather than watching it. I'd love a handsome, happy, horny orphan with a vasectomy, but I'm game for anything and enjoying the journey!

AND ANOTHER THING –
Revenge is utter crap. You might as well dig your own grave. We think your best bet is to live a full life by loving yourself and doing joyful and fun things. Besides, who wants to be someone's bitch –

IN THE SLAMMER?

"Go ahead, baby, let go of your old story –
REINVENT yourself."

– MJ and CB

Forgive yourself for being pissed.
Go through the "stages" of grief.
Face your fears of being alone or whatever your fears may be.
Say it all out loud. Write it down.
Be sad. Cry.
Then, when you're done …

GET OFF YOUR ASS

and choose to be happy! *Carpe diem,* as they say in Latin — seize the day!! Stop pussyfooting around.

We've given you a kick in the right direction. Now, go forth and prosper! Make us proud! Make yourselves proud!

Love,
MJ and CB

Acknowledgments

BIG KISSES TO:

Steve Ross, Director of the Book Division at Abrams Artists Agency-NY for believing in us; Mark Chimsky at Sellers Publishing for "getting" us; the amazing Sellers Team, especially Charlotte Cromwell's wonderful production work and the sexy sales peeps; the gorgeous and talented *DUMPED: The Trailer* stars — Michele Ammon, Nancy Meyer, Andrea Bianchi, Dana Vance, Michele Harris, Allegra Cohen, Alicia Harding, and Ilana Becker; our pal/sister/sounding board extraordinaire Pamela Fahey Middleton; our friends and CB's dad for sharing their experiences; our brilliant lawyer, Thomas J. FitzGerald; Josh Darden at Darden Studios; Eric Olsen at Process Type Foundry; Alexandra Rosa for our Anne Boleyn; and the following supportive kick-ass people: Gabriel Vaughan, Lesley Freedman Bailey, Judy Sternlight, Jennifer Grace Cook, John Wooten, Ruth McCullough, Harry Pritchett, Liz Klein, Marcus Villaca, Ariel Cepeda, Ann Abel, Mary Schafrath, Carolyn Fahey, SunHee Grinnell, Michael Hogan, Lewis Schiff, Amy Chamberlain, Corey Marsey, Michele Karas, Bill Tonelli, Laura Eisman, Wesley Alexander, Evelyne Pouget, Mitch Ditkoff, and Joe Thompson at Abrams Artists Agency-NY who walked DUMPED next door. WE LOVE YOU ALL!

MJ

To CB — for the tremendous good fortune of rediscovering each other. Thank you for your friendship, your energy, your loyalty, your smarts — and for the inexhaustible joy of working and being with you. To my pals, thanks for being in my corner! To my sisters Dolores and Carolyn and my brother, John, for the encouragement and love I thrive on. To the Bean, who is with me daily. To my mother, who taught us a whole lot about self-love. And finally, to my sister Pamela Fahey Middleton, for always being there.

CB

To MJ — my brainy, talented, seize-life-by-the-balls pal for life, I've enjoyed every minute of working/playing with you. I've had a blast gettin' off my ass and over my ex with you as my sidekick. To all of my fabulous friends, including the ones who dress like sluts and drink like fish at Happy Hour — I frickin' adore you all. To all my supportive, loving friends/family at Abrams Artists Agency-NY: Commercial, Voiceover & Print Divisions. . . .it's gonna be raining pickles, folks! To Dad, Mom, Brad, PJ, Petey, Steph, and Erica Lee for always being my #1 fans — love y'all!

WWW.DUMPED411.COM